SPIRIT WALK

STUDY GUIDE

L. Stone & Laura Smith

WILLIAM CAREY PUBLISHING

Available at missionbooks.org

Spirit Walk: Study Guide

© 2020 by L. Stone

For permission, email permissions@wclbooks.com. For corrections, email editor@wclbooks.com

Published by William Carey Publishing
10 W. Dry Creek Cir
Littleton, CO 80120 | www.missionbooks.org

William Carey Publishing is a ministry of Frontier Ventures
Pasadena, CA 91104 | www.frontierventures.org

Scripture quotations (unless otherwise noted) are taken from the ESV® Bible (The Holy Bible, English Standard Version®), copyright © 2001 by Crossway, a publishing ministry of Good News Publishers. Used by permission. All rights reserved.

Scripture quotations marked (NIV) are taken from the Holy Bible, New International Version®, NIV® Copyright © 1973, 1978, 1984, 2011 by Biblica, Inc.™ Used by permission of Zondervan. All rights reserved worldwide. www.zondervan.com. The "NIV" and "New International Version" are trademarks registered in the United States Patent and Trademark Office by Biblica, Inc.™

Cover and interior design: Mike Riester
Cover photo by Jasper Boer, unsplash.com
Senior editor: Melissa Hicks

ISBNs: 978-1-64508-335-1 (paperback), 978-1-64508-333-7 (mobi), 978-1-64508-334-4 (epub)

Worldwide distribution

24 23 22 21 20   1 2 3 4 5   IN

Library of Congress Control Number: 2020949827

CONTENTS

INTRODUCTION

The good news of the gospel is that the penalty for our sin has been paid by the sacrifice of Christ Jesus. We are no longer cast out of God's presence, but instead we have been invited into a real and intimate relationship with God through the indwelling power of the Holy Spirit. But what does that mean, practically? How do we walk in relationship with a Spirit that we cannot see and often don't know how to hear? What do the Scriptures teach us about how to cultivate this relationship so that our daily lives and ministries are marked by power from on high?

In *Spirit Walk*, Steve Smith searches the Scriptures to discover the path they lay out for walking in relationship with God through the Holy Spirit. But good doctrine alone concerning the Holy Spirit isn't enough. The Father desires worshipers who will worship Him in Spirit and in truth, not merely hearing truth, but putting it into practice!

Spirit Walk: Study Guide provides a daily homework structure that will challenge you to apply the truth you discover to not only understand who the Holy Spirit is, but to walk in greater intimacy with Him. It is through that intimacy that you will see His power demonstrated in your life and ministry. Blessings as you step out on your own Spirit Walk!

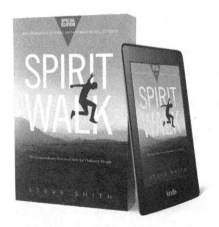

Spirit Walk (Special Edition)
available at missionbooks.org.

DAILY HOMEWORK STRUCTURE

Be Still Before the Lord—*2 minutes*

Worship the Lord with Thanksgiving—*3 minutes*

Invite the Lord to Speak to you—*1 minute*

Read *Spirit Walk*—*10–15 minutes*

Reflect & Respond—*5–15 minutes*

Be Still Before the Lord

Do not be quick with your mouth, do not be hasty in your heart to utter anything before God. God is in Heaven and you are on earth, so let your words be few.

—Ecclesiastes 5:2

It's impossible to walk with the Spirit daily without taking regular time to quiet our hearts and minds and be still before Him, giving Him our full attention. In a culture that increasingly values productivity, information and instant gratification, the discipline of stillness has all but disappeared. In order to be led by the Spirit of Jesus, we have to create space in our crazy lives to hear Him speak and to allow Him to move our hearts for what moves His. In the same way that we set aside time to invest intentionally in relationship with a spouse, we need to set aside intentional time to cultivate a relationship with the Holy Spirit. He is always available to us. He never leaves us or forsakes us. But how often during the day are we mindful of that reality?

Each day as we begin our time of reading and Bible study, we will take two minutes to sit before the Lord in silence, fixing our minds on Him. I often start this time by taking a deep breath and exhaling slowly or praying a short prayer, "Beloved, my eyes are fixed on you. Thank you for being here with me!"

At first, it may be difficult to quiet your mind. Your mind may race with concerns or things you need to accomplish. One way to fend off distractions is to adjust your posture. Kneel down. Stand with your face lifted to heaven. Cup your face in your hands. When distractions come, don't be discouraged. Simply dismiss the thoughts and re-center your attention on the Lord. It might be helpful to pray this short prayer again as you re-center your thoughts on the Lord. Some people find that playing a worship song in the background is helpful, but others are distracted by music. There is no formula. Find what best works for you. The important thing is that you are setting aside time just to be with Him.

During this time, the Holy Spirit may bring to mind unconfessed sin. If He does, confess it out loud. Confession isn't begging for forgiveness or even apologizing, it's simply agreeing with God about our sin. Confession brings sin into the light of God's presence so He can restore our hearts. I will never forget one night at midnight when I knelt on my living room floor unable to sleep. A little boy in my son's 2nd grade class had been bullying my child, and I was a mess over it. I simply said to the Lord, "God, I hate a seven-year-old boy." You see, there is no reason to hide the ugliness of our sin or to sugarcoat it. God knows our hearts already. Before I had time to apologize, the Holy Spirit spoke truth into my heart about the situation. In that moment a wave of compassion and peace swept over my heart washing away my sin. I spent a few more minutes praying for my son and for the other boy and his family, then went to bed and fell straight to sleep. Confession is powerful! I had been gripped by this hatred all day long, and a moment of confession in God's presence broke its power completely.

The more you practice the discipline of quieting your heart before the Lord and turning your gaze upon Him, the more it will become a natural part of your day. You will find yourself in a grocery store aisle, stuck in traffic or in the middle of your workday quieting your heart and turning your attention to the Lord. You will be more conscious of His presence with you! He is always speaking to us, convicting, comforting, and leading us into truth. We need only tune our ears to listen and incline our hearts to obey in order to receive from Him! As you get more comfortable being still and staying mindful of the Lord's presence, you may choose to spend longer or more frequent times of silence before Him.

Worship the Lord

We are not just reading a book to learn about God. We are setting aside time to receive conviction, encouragement and truth directly from the Holy Spirit. He WILL convict you, encourage you, comfort you and lead you into truth as you read and study! We want to be conscious of His presence with us as we read so the ears of our hearts are tuned to receive from Him. Scripture gives us a blueprint for coming into His presence.

Enter his gates with thanksgiving, and his courts with praise! —Psalm 100:4a

After taking time to be still before the Lord, take another few minutes to worship the Lord and to give thanks to Him. I would encourage you to pray out loud or journal your thoughts to keep your thoughts focused during this time. Instead of complaining or focusing on our problems, worship turns our attention to the greatness of God and thanksgiving calls to mind the goodness and love He has lavished on us!

There will be a suggested topic for your worship time each day, but feel free to worship the Lord however the Spirit leads you. You may choose to listen to a song, read a Psalm of praise or sing to the Lord a new song! Whatever you do, the point is to fix your eyes on Jesus, to declare His greatness and faithfulness and to fall more in love with Him as you do!

Invite the Lord to Speak to You

Each week there will be a prayer in the Study Guide for you to pray before reading that day's selection. Pray it whole-heartedly. As always, feel free to pray in your own words or as the Spirit leads you.

Read a Portion of *Spirit Walk*

Each day you will be encouraged to read a selection from the book *Spirit Walk*. **Do not skip this part of the homework.** The selections are fairly short, and you may choose to do all of the reading in one day. If you do, take time the following days to re-read sections of the chapters before answering the Reflect & Respond questions for those days. You will notice that different themes and Scriptures are repeated multiple times throughout the book. This is intentional! We have to meditate on a truth several times before it changes the way we think. None of the time you invest will be wasted!

Do not be conformed to this world, but be transformed by the renewal of your mind, that by testing you may discern what is the will of God, what is good and acceptable and perfect.
—Romans 12:2

Our goal throughout this study is to challenge our preconceived notions about the Holy Spirit and about life in Christ so that our lives are transformed by the renewing of our minds.

Reflect & Respond

Each day there will be a few questions to answer as you reflect on what the Lord spoke to you through the reading. Take the time to pray through each question and answer it thoughtfully.

As you work through these questions, set aside time to be quiet before the Lord again. Expect Him to speak to you during this time. Turn your attention to Him and ask Him what He wants to speak to you through what you read.

Just like we each have unique giftings, each of us hears from the Lord differently. Personally, I have never heard an audible voice, but many saints in both the old and new testaments did, so I will not rule it out! More often, God speaks to us through our conscious thoughts. After all, we have been given the mind of Christ! This is why it's important to journal our thoughts as we sit before Him. It's easy to quickly dismiss a thought, but if we take the time to write it down, the significance of it hits us in a new way.

Another way we often hear God speak is by being reminded of specific scriptures. If the Lord calls a scripture or even a biblical word to mind, look it up online or in your concordance and read scriptures that apply, asking the Lord to reveal more truth to your heart.

At other times, the Lord chooses to speak to us through our emotions. We sense His love for us or for someone else. We are overwhelmed by peace, or we feel His grief over brokenness. Sometimes, we are moved to tears by His presence as He reveals Himself to us. Our emotions are not always trustworthy, but the Holy Spirit is. If He uses your emotions to reveal something to you,

don't discount it. Ask Him to clarify what He is showing you through His word of truth.

When waiting on the Lord, some people will have clear, powerful, short phrases that repeat in their thoughts. Others have pictures or stories come to mind. The Holy Spirit can use these things just like Jesus used pictures and parables throughout the gospels. If the Lord speaks to you this way, continue to sit before Him asking Him to also reveal the broader meaning and application of those phrases or pictures. Take time to look up relevant passages of Scripture and meditate on the truths the Holy Spirit is calling to mind.

Remember the Holy Spirit is called the spirit of wisdom, comfort and encouragement. His kindness draws us to repentance. Like Adam and Eve, our natural tendency is to hide from the presence of God when we become aware of our sin. But when the Holy Spirit reveals sin or immaturity in your life, He is speaking to you because He loves you. He wants you to draw near to Him to be restored! Run to His presence so He can transform you by His power. If you feel condemned, inadequate or discouraged, take those thoughts captive. Satan is called the "accuser of the brethren." He tells you that you are not worthy and that you have no business coming into God's presence. Who are you to think God would speak to you? He wants you to feel like you are not qualified to hear from God or to be used by Him. He is a liar! If the Holy Spirit dwells in you, you have the power to stop entertaining those thoughts and to choose instead to meditate on truth.

If the Holy Spirit convicts you about sin or wrong beliefs, confess it immediately, out loud, and receive His forgiveness.

Make a plan to obey Him right away. Share your plan with a trusted friend who will keep you accountable to follow through in the coming days and weeks.

1 Corinthians tells us that the manifestation of the Spirit is given for the common good, to edify the body of Christ. If the Holy Spirit leads you to encourage or serve a brother or sister in Christ, obey right away. If you feel uncomfortable or uncertain about how to do that, ask a mentor or Bible study leader for wisdom, but don't grieve the Spirit by letting the opportunity to be a part of what He is doing pass you by.

If you sense the Lord calling you into new areas of surrender in your life or leading you to partner with His mission in your generation in new ways, make a plan to obey Him right away. Share your plan with someone who will encourage you to follow through. Then continue seeking Him in the days and weeks that come.

> *I am the vine; you are the branches. Whoever abides in me and I in him, he it is that bears much fruit, for apart from me you can do nothing.* —John 15:5

In order to be fruitful in what God is calling you to do, you will have to stay connected to Him, receiving life-giving power from the vine daily. God does not ask you to do something for Him and then say, "Go ahead and do it on your own." God has designed you to depend on Him for the strength and power you need to accomplish His purposes.

As we seek to grow in our maturity to perceive the promptings of the Holy Spirit and to respond in obedience, the Word of God grounds us. If you ever have questions about what you think the Lord is speaking to you, ask a trusted friend or Bible study leader who can help you discern if it agrees with the Word of God. The Word of God is our ultimate guide in discerning truth.

> *For the word of God is living and active, sharper than any two-edged sword, piercing to the division of soul and of spirit, of joints and of marrow, and discerning the thoughts and intentions of the heart. And no creature is hidden from his sight, but all are naked and exposed to the eyes of him to whom we must give account.* —Hebrews 4:12–13

The Holy Spirit of God is a trustworthy counselor, but the Bible helps us discern between the trustworthy leadings of the Holy Spirit and our own unreliable emotions and deceptive human reasoning.

Weekly Bible Study

> *Let the word of Christ dwell in you richly, teaching and admonishing one another in all wisdom.* —Colossians 3:16a

On day five of each week, we will meditate on a specific passage of Scripture. Every week our reading will reference multiple passages of Scripture. Take time to read and re-read them. After you complete the reading each week, choose a specific Scripture from the selected text to study on your own. Allow the Spirit to be your guide. The Lord may lead you to a particular verse for any reason: perhaps it encourages you, challenges the way you think, convicts you or just confuses you and makes you want to understand more. Feel free to study scriptures outside of our reading as well. Remember, the Spirit Walk is about responding to the Holy Spirit's unpredictable promptings, fearlessly! Trust Him as He leads.

After you have selected a passage of Scripture to study, look it up in your Bible and read it in context. Read the full chapter, observing who wrote it and to whom it was written and noting the purpose for which it was written.

You may also want to read it in another translation. This Study Guide has space to write the passage you choose to study and questions to work through as you study that passage on your own.

NOTES   **Introduction**

Session 1 | RETURNING TO A BIBLICAL FRAMEWOR

| **DAY 1** | If you have not already done so, start by reading the **Introduction** to this Study Guide. |

Be Still Before the Lord (2 minutes)

Worship the Lord

For the word of the LORD is upright, and all his work is done in faithfulness. He loves righteousness and justice; the earth is full of the steadfast love of the Lord.

—Psalm 33:4–5

Turn to Psalm 33 in your Bible. Read the chapter aloud, pausing after each verse to meditate on the greatness of God and fall more in love with Him!

Invite God to Speak to You Today

"Father, I want to worship you in spirit and in truth because you said that is the kind of worship that delights you. As I seek you today, I ask you to reveal anything I have believed about your Holy Spirit that isn't true. Banish every fear. Reveal any cultural bias, misunderstanding or apathy that has taken root in my life. I want to know YOU as you really are! Awaken my heart to the reality of your Spirit at work all around me and give me a heart that longs to know You and please You more and more!"

Read a Portion of *Spirit Walk*

If you have *Spirit Walk (Special Edition)*, read the **Foreword** by Steve Smith and answer the following questions. If not, you may skip to the next section.

1. Has the weight of your sin and shame been lifted and have you joyfully entered into a relationship with the Father like Steve describes? If so, describe what changed in your heart and life when you first received God's forgiveness and love.

2. Take an honest assessment of your life. There is no shame in being brutally honest. You have been accepted as a child of God because of the righteouness of Christ, not your own goodness. Transformation begins with honest confession and brokenness! Would you say Jesus is an important part of your life or do you truly obey Him unconditionally as your Master?

3. To what extent do you walk in the power of the Holy Spirit day by day?

Reflect & Respond

Please read the **Preface** of *Spirit Walk* and answer the following questions:

1. How does the analogy of the Holy Spirit being like wind enhance your understanding of the Spirit's nature and His work?

2. If there are two types of believers, those who fail to see or hear the Wind and those who allow the Wind to engulf them, which are you and why do you think that is?

3. What emotions are stirred up when you read about the work of the Holy Spirit and when you consider inviting Him to engulf your life?

Depending on your personal experience or faith tradition, talk of the Holy Spirit might elicit anticipation and hope or, alternatively, inadequacy, anxiety or confusion. For many, the Holy Spirit is the undervalued and largely misunderstood third person of the Trinity, but, according to Jesus, His presence brings peace, wisdom, and power. We definitely don't need to be protecting ourselves from the Spirit of Jesus.

4. Take some time to ask the Lord if there is anything you have believed about the Spirit of God that isn't TRUE. Write a prayer confessing any anxiety or misunderstandings and inviting God to teach you about Himself as we study His word together.

DAY 2

Be Still Before the Lord (2 minutes)

Worship the Lord

"If anyone thirsts, let him come to me and drink. Whoever believes in me, as the Scripture has said, 'Out of his heart will flow rivers of living water.'" Now this he said about the Spirit, whom those who believed in him were to receive, for as yet the Spirit had not been given, because Jesus was not yet glorified. —John 7:37b–39

Spend some time worshipping Jesus who has now been glorified and sits at the right hand of the throne of God in heaven. Thank Him for sending His Spirit to be with us and to be in us.

Invite God to Speak to You Today

"Father, I want to worship you in spirit and in truth because you said that is the kind of worship that delights you. As I seek you today, I ask you to reveal anything I have believed about your Holy Spirit that isn't true. Banish every fear. Reveal any cultural bias, misunderstanding or apathy that has taken root in my life. I want to know YOU as you really are! Awaken my heart to the reality of your Spirit at work all around me and give me a heart that longs to know you and to please you more and more!"

Read a Portion of *Spirit Walk*

Read the **Introduction**.

Reflect & Respond

1. Do you regularly see the extraordinary power of the Spirit of God that we have just read about at work in your life? Are you content with your current experience of God's power?

2. The Bible encourages us to live in relationship with God through His Holy Spirit, but "Holy Spirit illiteracy abounds even among long time Christians." Instead of walking in relationship with Him, our tendency is to keep Him at a distance, to resort to our own control or to substitute predictable props and programs for the unpredictable guide. How do you see these tendencies in your own life?

- Keeping the Holy Spirit at a distance

- Resorting to your own control

- Substituting programs or props for reliance upon the Holy Spirit

3. Write the four spiritual disciplines of the Spirit Walk in your own words.

S _____

W _____

A _____

P _____

4. If you are a child of God, you have received the Holy Spirit. Chances are He has already been using these spiritual disciplines to teach you. Use the space below to describe how you understand each of these spiritual disciplines and how the Lord has used them in your life already.

5. Circle the spiritual discipline you need to grow in the most. What do you think has kept you from maturing in this discipline in the past? How do you think the Lord might use this posture to help you mature in your walk with Him?

6. Take a moment and ask the Lord to show you how you have grieved the Holy Spirit by keeping Him at a distance, relying on your own strength or substituting church service or activities for a love relationship with Him. When you are done, write a prayer of confession and invite the Holy Spirit to teach you a new way of loving Him as you walk through this study.

DAY 3

Be Still Before the Lord (2 minutes)

Worship the Lord

"Not by might, nor by power, but by my Spirit," says the LORD of hosts.

—Zechariah 4:6b

What a privilege to be free to rely on the almighty power of the LORD of hosts! Spend some time meditating on the incomparably great power of God and worshiping Him for making His power available for those who believe! As you worship, call to mind some of the mighty things God has done in Scripture and in your own life.

Invite the Lord to Speak to You

"Father, I want to worship you in spirit and in truth because you said that is the kind of worship that delights you. As I seek you today, I ask you to reveal anything I have believed about your Holy Spirit that isn't true. Banish every fear. Reveal any cultural bias, misunderstanding or apathy that has taken root in my life. I want to know YOU as you really are! Awaken my heart to the reality of your Spirit at work all around me and give me a heart that longs to know you and please you more and more!"

Read a Portion of *Spirit Walk*

Read Chapter 1, **Predictable Steps for an Unpredictable Path** through **The Turning Point in Every Historical Awakening**.

Chapters in *Spirit Walk* are divided into several smaller sections. Each day, read from the beginning of the first section, or in this case the beginning of the chapter through the end of the second section indicated.

Reflect & Respond

1. Have you experienced biblical paths and discipleship processes that felt "devoid of power?" Give an example.

2. Have you ever started out on a good path in God's power and then fizzled out because you took back control or started depending on your own strength?

3. Being led and empowered by the Holy Spirit has always been the Biblical Plan A for followers of Jesus. Oftentimes, however, there's a lack of discipleship on how to live that out. Reflect on your own experience in the body of Christ. Have you ever been discipled in what it means to live according to the Spirit or to be empowered by Him? If so, are you continuing to be led by the Spirit daily and discipling others? Why do you think that is?

4. Are you willing to take the predictable and Biblical steps to be led by the Spirit of God down an unpredictable path?

DAY 4

Be Still Before the Lord (2 minutes)

Worship the Lord

The Spirit of the Lord is upon me, because he has anointed me to proclaim good news to the poor.

He has sent me to proclaim liberty to the captives and recovering of sight to the blind, to set at liberty those who are oppressed, to proclaim the year of the Lord's favor.

—Luke 4:18–19

Has the Lord spoken good news to you? Has He set you free? Has He given you eyes to see? Take time today to worship the Lord like it is the only chance you will get to tell Him how much you love Him and to thank Him for all that He has done for you.

Invite God to Speak to You Today

"Lord, I want to know YOU as you really are! Awaken my heart to the reality of your Spirit at work all around me and give me a heart that longs to know you more every day! I want to love you more today than I loved you yesterday. And I want to love you more tomorrow than I do today. Lord, give me a heart of worship and speak to me through your Word, today, I pray."

Read a Portion of *Spirit Walk*

Read Chapter 1, **Banishing Fear** through the end of the chapter.

Reflect & Respond

1. What fears or misconceptions have kept you from fully embracing the Spirit's leadership? How has the reading today changed your understanding?

2. If you have trusted Christ as your Savior, the Spirit dwells within you. Do you know if He has ever filled you (for the first time or a fifty-first time)?

3. Since yesterday's filling is no guarantee of today's filling, are you full of the Spirit today? Would you like to be?

4. What steps can you take today to get started in your Spirit Walk?

5. Write a prayer now asking the Lord for courage to take this path!

DAY 5

Be Still Before the Lord (2 minutes)

Worship the Lord

For since the creation of the world God's invisible qualities—his eternal power and divine nature—have been clearly seen, being understood from what has been made, so that people are without excuse. —Romans 1:20 (NIV)

Spend time worshipping God for revealing His beauty and might through creation. Take time to look outside. Observe how intricately each cloud and plant has been made. Listen to the sounds of birds and insects. Feel the warmth of the sun or the cool of the wind on your face. What a mighty and beautiful God we serve!

Invite the Lord to Speak to You Today

"Lord, I want to know YOU as you really are! Awaken my heart to the reality of your Spirit at work all around me and give me a heart that longs to know you more every day! I want to love you more today than I loved you yesterday. And I want to love you more tomorrow than I do today. Lord, give me a heart of worship and speak to me through your Word, today, I pray."

Bible Study

Select a Scripture from this week's reading to study, and write the full verse(s) below.

1. Turn to the verse in your Bible and read it in the context of the full chapter. Does reading it in context, or in another translation, add to your understanding of this passage? If so, how?

2. Look up any key words that may help you gain a deeper understanding of the passage.

3. Ask the Lord, "What do you specifically want to speak to me through this passage today?"

4. Does this passage challenge any assumptions you have about "Living according to the Holy Spirit?"

5. What truth does this Scripture reveal about God, and how can it move you to worship Him today?

6. What does this Scripture reveal about you and/or humanity in general?

7. Ask the Lord, "Would you show me if there is any wrong belief or sin in my heart that has kept me from living in conformity with this Scripture?"

8. What practical steps of obedience will you take today in response to this passage?

9. Who will you tell something you learned from this passage?

10. Write a prayer in your journal thanking God for what He is teaching you and asking Him for the courage to surrender to Him completely.

Session 1 NOTES **Returning To A Biblical Framework**

BEING FILLED WITH THE HOLY SPIRIT

DAY 1

Be Still Before the Lord (2 minutes)

Worship the Lord

For as high as the heavens are above the earth, so great is his steadfast love toward those who fear him . . . —Psalm 103:11

Turn to Psalm 103 in your Bible and read the whole chapter, pausing to meditate on each verse and to worship the Lord for His greatness!

Invite God to Speak to You Today

Don't rush through this time each day. Prayer isn't something we do quickly so we can get on to more productive endeavors. It is the lifeblood of our time with God. The author of Hebrews challenges us to come boldly before the Lord. SO come boldly today! You have been given an audience with the King of Kings and a position of privilege as His child. Wow! Ask Him confidently for the Holy Spirit's help as you read and as you study His word. Luke 11:13 tells us that it is His delight to give the Holy Spirit to His children who ask. He will do it! Mother Teresa used to frequently pray, "that I may love God with a love with which He has never been loved before." This week, let's echo that prayer together.

"Lord, I don't just want to know about you, I want to have a loving relationship with you. Father, I have loved so many things, but move my heart to love YOU more than anything else. Oh, LORD, give me a heart that loves you like you've never been loved before. Only you could do that kind of work in my heart."

Read a Portion of *Spirit Walk*

Read Chapter 2, **Spirit Walk** through **Letting the Word of Christ Richly Dwell Within You**. In this selection we discussed 3 different phrases that Scripture uses to describe the process of walking with the Holy Spirit.

Abiding in Christ,

being filled with the Holy Spirit,

letting the Word of Christ richly dwell in you richly.

In the West, we like to think of things linearly and systematically, but the Spirit Walk is neither of those. It is a relationship with a living person, the Holy Spirit of Jesus. Jesus often spoke in stories and pictures in order to bypass our systematic way of thinking and connect with our hearts. That is what the Scriptures are doing for us here. All 3 of these phrases refer to the same process, but each analogy deepens our understanding in a unique way. As we reflect on these pictures, ask the Holy Spirit to use each one to bring clarity, conviction and encouragement not only to your mind but in your heart!

Reflect & Respond

1. How does thinking about the Holy Spirit as the Spirit of Jesus help you as you think about the Spirit Walk?

2. **Abiding in Christ**

   • How does the analogy of abiding clarify your understanding of the Spirit Walk?

   • Is the Holy Spirit using this picture to bring conviction or point out ways you could grow in your Spirit Walk?

   • Does the Lord's promise to abide with you encourage your heart today?

3. **Being Filled with the Spirit**

   - How does the analogy of being filled clarify your understanding of the Spirit Walk?

   - Is the Holy Spirit using this picture to point out ways you could grow in your Spirit Walk?

   - How does the Lord's desire to fill you encourage your heart uniquely?

4. **Letting the Word of Christ richly dwell in you**

   - How does the analogy of the Word dwelling in you clarify your understanding of the Spirit Walk?

   - How is the Holy Spirit using this picture to point out unique ways you could grow in your Spirit Walk?

   - Describe how this analogy encourages your heart?

5. Take some time to respond to the conviction of the Holy Spirit in prayer. Make a plan to obey Him then worship Him for the ways He has encouraged you through His word today.

DAY 2

Be Still Before the Lord (2 minutes)

Worship the Lord

And let the peace of Christ rule in your hearts, to which indeed you were called in one body. And be thankful. Let the word of Christ dwell in you richly, teaching and admonishing one another in all wisdom, singing psalms and hymns and spiritual songs, with thankfulness in your hearts to God. —Colossians 3:15–16

Have you been tempted to complain about anything recently? Is there anything stealing your peace? Complaining and worry are the opposite of worship. Spend some time today turning these struggles into a prayer of thanksgiving and singing praise to the Lord!

Invite God to Speak to You Today

"Lord, I don't just want to know about you, I want to have a loving relationship with you. Father, I have loved so many things, but move my heart to love YOU more than anything else. Oh, LORD, give me a heart that loves you like you've never been loved before. Only you could do that kind of work in my heart."

Read a Portion of *Spirit Walk*

Read Chapter 2, **Keeping in Step With the Spirit** through the end of the chapter.

Reflect & Respond

1. Galatians 5:25 encourages us to keep in step with the Spirit. How does the analogy of the guide on your journey add to your understanding of the Spirit Walk?

2. How well have you been doing letting the Holy Trailblazer guide you on your journey? Has the Holy Spirit pointed out new ways that you could grow in your walk with Him today?

3. What specific changes would you like to make? Is there someone that you are journeying with whom you could ask to hold you accountable to make these changes?

4. The Lord of the dance is inviting you to walk in step with Him. Take time now. Write a prayer inviting Him to teach you the steps. Surrender to Him as your King.

DAY 3

Be Still Before the Lord (2 minutes)

Worship the Lord

But the fruit of the Spirit is love, joy, peace, patience, kindness, goodness, faithfulness, gentleness, self-control; against such things there is no law. —Galatians 5:22–23

Have you ever considered that the Holy Spirit can give us power to be loving, patient, gentle and self-controlled because God is all of these things? Spend some time worshipping God for exemplifying each of these virtues. Think of ways He has demonstrated these things in Scripture or in your life. Thank Him for sending us the Holy Spirit to empower us to be like Him in these ways!

Invite God to Speak to You Today

"Lord, I don't just want to know about you, I want to have a loving relationship with you. Father, I have loved so many things, but move my heart to love YOU more than anything else. Oh, LORD, give me a heart that loves you like you've never been loved before. Only you could do that kind of work in my heart."

Read a Portion of *Spirit Walk*

Read Chapter 3, **S.W.A.P. Your Control for God's.**

Reflect & Respond

1. Why is it helpful to think about your relationship with the Spirit as a perfect marriage?

2. What have you learned in marriage, or through the marriages of others, that might help you as you think about developing a daily relationship with the Holy Spirit?

3. If you want a really good "marriage" with the Holy Spirit, how are you willing to work on your part as a partner? Are you willing to make the changes in your relationship that He reveals to you?

4. If you were to view your relationship with God as a marriage, what kind of marriage would you currently have? For what it's worth, God is always faithful. If the relationship is strained, it's on us! Take some time to pray and to write out goals for how you desire to grow in your "marriage" relationship with the Lord.

DAY 4

Be Still Before the Lord (2 minutes)

Worship the Lord

Let the wicked forsake his way, and the unrighteous man his thoughts; let him return to the LORD, that he may have compassion on him, and to our God, for he will abundantly pardon. For my thoughts are not your thoughts, neither are your ways my ways, declares the LORD. For as the heavens are higher than the earth, so are my ways higher than your ways and my thoughts than your thoughts.

—Isaiah 55:7–9

The relationship God invites us to have with Him is mysterious! His thoughts and His ways are so much higher than ours. For a human to love like He does would be considered reckless. Spend some time worshipping the Lord who continually has compassion on us and abundantly pardons our unfaithfulness! Ask Him to remind you of specific instances in which He freely pardoned you and remained faithful to His relationship with you, even though you were unfaithful.

Invite God to Speak to You Today

"Lord, I don't just want to know about you, I want to have a loving relationship with you. Father, I have loved so many things, but move my heart to love YOU more than anything else. Oh, LORD, give me a heart that loves you like you've never been loved before. Only you could do that kind of work in my heart."

Read a Portion of *Spirit Walk*

There is no new reading for today, but feel free to look back over the sections we have read as you prepare to Reflect & Respond.

Reflect & Respond

1. S.W.A.P. describes four biblical activities that help you build a better marriage with the Spirit. Let's review them. Describe what each of these mean to you at this point in our journey.

   S _____

   W _____

A _____

P _____

2. How hungry are you for God and His control over your life? If you are not feeling hungry, are you willing to be hungry?

3. What fears or concerns do you have? Be prepared to share this with your small group and to encourage each other.

4. Ask God now to create a deep hunger for Him and for you to do your part to create the ideal spiritual marriage. Consider writing a prayer in your journal or getting on your face before God and crying out to Him. We cannot do this in our own strength. We need His strength to love and obey Him faithfully. We even need His strength to WANT to do it!

DAY 5

Be Still Before the Lord (2 minutes)

Worship the Lord

All we like sheep have gone astray; we have turned—every one—to his own way; and the Lord has laid on him the iniquity of us all. —Isaiah 53:6

None of us has done a perfect job keeping in step with the Holy Spirit as our guide. Most of us have actually done a pretty terrible job following Him, but He has been so patient with us. Spend some time thanking the Lord for His patience and forbearance with you when you have gone astray and done things your own way. Thank Him for Jesus! Thank Him for His presence with you today despite all of the times you have disregarded Him as your guide.

Invite the Lord to Speak to You Today

"Lord, I don't just want to know about you, I want to have a loving relationship with you. Father, I have loved so many things, but move my heart to love YOU more than anything else! Oh, LORD, give me a heart that loves you like you've never been loved before. Only you could do that kind of work in my heart!"

Bible Study

Select a Scripture from this week's reading to study, and write the full verse(s) below.

1. Turn to the verse in your Bible and read it in the context of the full chapter. Does reading it in context, or in another translation, add to your understanding of this passage? If so, how?

2. Look up any key words that may help you gain a deeper understanding of the passage.

3. Ask the Lord, "What do you specifically want to speak to me through this passage today?"

4. Does this passage challenge any assumptions you have about "Living according to the Holy Spirit?"

5. What truth does this Scripture reveal about God, and how can it move you to worship Him today?

6. What does this Scripture reveal about you and/or humanity in general?

7. Ask the Lord, "Would you show me if there is any wrong belief or sin in my heart that has kept me from living in conformity with this Scripture?"

8. What practical steps of obedience will you take today in response to this passage?

9. Who will you tell something you learned from this passage?

10. Write a prayer in your journal thanking God for what He is teaching you and asking Him for the courage to surrender to Him completely.

Session 3 | SURRENDER

DAY 1

Be Still Before the Lord (2 minutes)

How are you doing being still before the Lord? Is this time each day fruitful? If not, take some time to re-read the *Study Guide* **Introduction** section on Being Still Before the Lord (page 4). Consider changing things up or starting with worship instead of stillness. God is always present with you. The goal of this time is to help you grow in your awareness of His presence and in being present relationally with Him.

Worship the Lord

> *Your kingdom is an everlasting kingdom, and your dominion endures throughout all generations. The LORD is faithful in all his words and kind in all his works.*
>
> —Psalm 145:13

Turn to Psalm 145 in your Bible. Read it aloud, declaring the goodness and power of our God. He is so worthy of praise! Who can fathom His greatness?

Invite God to Speak to You Today

"Beloved, I choose YOU. I want to be completely yours. Give me the courage to surrender to you in every area of my life. Show me how I can surrender to you more fully today."

Read a Portion of *Spirit Walk*

Read Chapter 4, **S.W.A.P.—Surrender to His Will and Word** through **Four Commands in the S.W.A.P. Framework.**

Reflect & Respond

1. We live in a culture that honors independence and pride as virtues and views surrender as weakness or even failure. But the kingdom of God turns things upside down. Ask the Lord, "How is my thinking about surrender and control influenced by my culture or my family history?"

2. Surrender is meant to be a posture of our hearts in the same way that LOVE is the determined posture of God's heart toward us. Is your heart posture toward God one of surrender? Are you letting God control and fill you in each moment? Explain.

3. Are there rooms in your heart to which you haven't given the Holy Spirit the keys? Describe those rooms.

4. Are there areas in your life where it has been painful to hand over complete control to the Lord? Why have you wanted to maintain control of these areas? Ask the Lord, "God, why do I feel like I cannot give you control of this?" Write your thoughts and anything He reveals to you in the space provided.

DAY 2

Be Still Before the Lord (2 minutes)

Worship the Lord

"For I have come down from heaven, not to do my own will but the will of him who sent me."

"For this is the will of my Father, that everyone who looks on the Son and believes in him should have eternal life, and I will raise him up on the last day."

—John 6:38, 40

Spend some time declaring the kindness and greatness of Jesus, who was willing to surrender completely to His Father's will so that you could be in relationship with God. Surrender is HARD. It was not easy or painless for Jesus, but it's because He was tempted in every way and yet was without sin that He can empower us by His Spirit to live lives of surrender.

Invite God to Speak to You Today

"Beloved, I choose YOU. I want to be completely yours. Give me the courage to surrender to you in every area of my life. Show me how I can surrender to you more fully today."

Read a Portion of *Spirit Walk*

Read Chapter 4, **Surrender Not Commitment** through **Can You Trust God**.

Reflect & Respond

1. How is *surrender* different from *commitment*? Are you committed to God or are you surrendered to Him?

2. Are you willing to sign the blank paper of surrender? If not, pray the most honest prayer of your life, right now. Tell the Lord exactly where you are with this. Don't hold back. You don't need to play games with Him. He knows already, and He has chosen to love you and to fight for your heart!

3. Trusting in the goodness and loving kindness of God is foundational for surrendering to Him. What needs to change in your perspective on God's goodness in order for you to be willing to surrender to Him?

DAY 3

Be Still Before the Lord (2 minutes)

Worship the Lord

For I am sure that neither death nor life, nor angels nor rulers, nor things present nor things to come, nor powers, nor height nor depth, nor anything else in all creation, will be able to separate us from the love of God in Christ Jesus our Lord.
—Romans 8:38–39

But God, being rich in mercy, because of the great love with which he loved us, even when we were dead in our trespasses, made us alive together with Christ—by grace you have been saved—and raised us up with him and seated us with him in the heavenly places in Christ Jesus, so that in the coming ages he might show the immeasurable riches of his grace in kindness toward us in Christ Jesus.
—Ephesians 2:4–7

See what kind of love the Father has given to us, that we should be called children of God; and so we are. The reason why the world does not know us is that it did not know him.
—1 John 3:1

Spend some time meditating on and receiving God's great love for you. Write a prayer of thanksgiving expressing your love for Him.

Invite God to Speak to You Today

"Beloved, I choose YOU. I want to be completely yours. Give me the courage to surrender to you in every area of my life. Show me how I can surrender to you more fully today."

Read a Portion of *Spirit Walk*

Read Chapter 4, **Surrender to His Will** through **The Great Commission Promise.**

Reflect & Respond

1. How well are you surrendered to the will and mission of God?

2. Have you ever unconditionally surrendered yourself to the Lord, no matter what He said? If so, what did that look like?

3. Describe a time when you were living for God's mission and you experienced His power and presence in a palpable way?

4. Read Matthew 16:24–27. In light of our reading today, what does this passage mean to you?

Before putting away the study today, ask the Lord to search your heart and change the way you think about surrender. Pray this prayer whole-heartedly or write your own.

"Father, open the eyes of my heart to see how this applies to my life. I want to see it the way you do. Father, show me the value of my comfort and how that compares to the opportunity to know you and to see you move in mighty ways through my life."

DAY 4

Be Still Before the Lord (2 minutes)

Worship the Lord

The word of the LORD came to Jeremiah: "Behold, I am the Lord, the God of all flesh. Is anything too hard for me?" —Jeremiah 32:26–27

Read Jeremiah's prayer in Jeremiah 32:17–25. Jeremiah recounts the great things God has done for him and for the people of Israel, and he cries out to God to rescue them again from the army surrounding them. Spoiler alert: It does not end well for the Israelites this time. God chose to let them endure the consequences of their rebellion. Nevertheless, take some time to write your own prayer recalling the great things God has done for you and asking him to display His great power in your current situation. Nothing is too hard for Him!

Invite God to Speak to You Today

"Beloved, I choose YOU. I want to be completely yours. Give me the courage to surrender to you in every area of my life. Show me how I can surrender to you more fully today."

Read a Portion of *Spirit Walk*

Read Chapter 4, **Surrender to His Every Word** through the end of the chapter.

Reflect & Respond

1. What challenges do you face in surrendering to every WORD of Christ—every "honey-will-you?"

2. Take time now to pull out a fresh, blank sheet of paper. If it expresses your heart, sign your name at the bottom and tell God,

   "Father, You love me unconditionally. I trust You to guide my life. I surrender to Your control. Write on here any directions for this week, this month, this year, this life. I am Yours!"

DAY 5

Be Still Before the Lord (2 minutes)

Worship the Lord

The heart of man plans his way, but the LORD establishes his steps.
—Proverbs 16:9

How has God directed your paths in the past? Spend some time calling these things to mind and thanking Him. Then worship Him that He holds all the days in your future, as well. Think of the people close to you and worship the Lord for doing the same things for them.

Invite God to Speak to You Today

"Beloved, I choose YOU. I want to be completely yours. Give me the courage to surrender to you in every area of my life. Show me how I can surrender to you more fully today."

Read a Portion of *Spirit Walk*

Read Chapter 4, **Surrender to His Every Word** through the end of the chapter.

Bible Study

Select a Scripture from this week's reading to study, and write the full verse(s) below.

1. Turn to the verse in your Bible and read it in the context of the full chapter. Does reading it in context, or in another translation, add to your understanding of this passage? If so, how?

2. Look up any key words that may help you gain a deeper understanding of the passage.

3. Ask the Lord, "What do you specifically want to speak to me through this passage today?"

4. Does this passage challenge any assumptions you have about "Living according to the Holy Spirit?"

5. What truth does this Scripture reveal about God, and how can it move you to worship Him today?

6. What does this Scripture reveal about you and/or humanity in general?

7. Ask the Lord, "Would you show me if there is any wrong belief or sin in my heart that has kept me from living in conformity with this Scripture?"

8. What practical steps of obedience will you take today in response to this passage?

9. Who will you tell something you learned from this passage?

10. Write a prayer in your journal thanking God for what He is teaching you and asking Him for the courage to surrender to Him completely.

Surrender

WAITING ON GOD

DAY 1

Be Still Before the Lord (2 minutes)

Worship the Lord

One thing have I asked of the LORD, that will I seek after: that I may dwell in the house of the LORD all the days of my life,
to gaze upon the beauty of the LORD and to inquire in his temple. —Psalm 27:4

When David wrote these words, Jesus had not yet been glorified, and the Holy Spirit had not yet come. Today, you possess God's generous response to David's request. If you are in Christ, you may freely dwell in His temple all the days of your life. The Holy Spirit has not only given you access, but He is present with you to reveal to you the beauty of the Father and the Son!

The Lord inhabits the praises of His people. You don't have to experience His presence emotionally to be confident that He hears you and that He is present with you. Meditate on this truth today and express your gratitude to the Lord. Spend some time enjoying the LORD's presence and gazing on His beauty today before you go any further.

Invite God to Speak to You Today

"Lord, It's scary to give my life fully to your purposes! As I seek you today, stir my affection for you. Break my heart for the things that break your heart. Give me a hunger to live for you and your purposes. Thank you for moving in mighty ways in my generation. Show me how I can join you in what you are doing today."

Read a Portion of *Spirit Walk*

Read Chapter 5, **S.W.A.P.—Wait on God in Prayer** through **Prayer to Glorify God.**

Reflect & Respond

> *"The Father seeks fervent worshippers who will bring glory to Him. To worship Him, He requires you to align your will and thinking to His. He is not in the business of aligning His will and thinking to yours. He is God, and you are not."*
>
> —*Spirit Walk (Special Edition)*

Sometimes we think that we are "waiting on God," but in reality, we are just waiting for God to align His thinking and desires with our own and give us what we want. In these seasons we likely are not willing to hear Him say anything to us until He gives us what we want. This always ends in disappointment!

1. Have you ever been disappointed in God because He didn't do what you wanted Him to do? Have you ever thought He was silent because He wasn't saying want you wanted to hear? Explain.

2. I know this is tender, but for some of us, it will be all too real. Disappointment in God grieves the Holy Spirit. It can put a riff in your relationship that needs to be healed for you to be free to receive from Him afresh.

   • Spend some time asking the Lord to show you if you've believed something about Him that isn't true because He did not meet YOUR expectations. Pour out your heart to Him. He loves you.

   • Ask the Lord to forgive you and to enable you to trust his goodness and sovereignty over your life. Write a prayer in your journal declaring your trust in Him.

   • Invite the Holy Spirit to align your desires and thoughts with His and to fill you afresh with His Spirit.

3. I think most of us will agree that doing things for God feels more natural than waiting on God. Waiting seems unproductive but waiting on God is NOT a passive posture. Describe how waiting on God can be both productive and intentional.

4. God has invited you to be His vessel, to live in His power and to reveal His glory! This is bigger than anything you've ever imagined. What an incredible privilege! But in order to do this, you have to BE CLOTHED with power from on high.

   • Set aside a chunk of time today to wait on the Lord in prayer. Get on your knees or on your face. Read again through the **Prayer to Glorify God** in Chapter 5. Write a prayer of your own, asking God to do what only He can do through your life!

DAY 2

Be Still Before the Lord (2 minutes)

Worship the Lord

The LORD sits enthroned over the flood; the LORD sits enthroned as king forever.
May the LORD give strength to his people!
May the LORD bless his people with peace!

—Psalm 29:10–11

Turn to Psalm 29 and read the whole chapter. Meditate on His great power and sovereignty. How beautiful it is that the same God whose voice breaks the cedars speaks peace over His people!

Invite God to Speak to You Today

"Lord, It's scary to give my life fully to your purposes! As I seek you today, stir my affection for you. Break my heart for the things that break your heart. Give me a hunger to live for you and your purposes. Thank you for moving in mighty ways in my generation. Show me how I can join you in what you are doing today."

Read a Portion of *Spirit Walk*

Read Chapter 5, **Prayer of Confession** through the end of the chapter.

Reflect & Respond

1. What are the biggest messages God has spoken to you while reading about the waiting-in-prayer process described in this chapter?

2. Re-read the **Prayer of Confession** in chapter 5 of *Spirit Walk*. Set aside some time to get still before the Lord and write your own prayer of confession, or pray through this one whole-heartedly.

3. Is there a need to take a period of time and to fast for breakthrough? Pause for a moment and ask the Lord to lead you as you consider this question then set aside some time to wait and listen before answering the questions below.

   • What will you fast from?

   • How long will you fast?

   • Who are you inviting to hold you accountable?

   • Who are you inviting to fast with you?

DAY 3

Be Still Before the Lord (2 minutes)

Worship the Lord

Oh, the depth of the riches of the wisdom and knowledge of God!
How unsearchable his judgments, and his paths beyond tracing out!
"Who has known the mind of the Lord? Or who has been his counselor?"
"Who has ever given to God, that God should repay them?" For from him and
through him and for him are all things. To him be the glory forever! Amen.

—Romans 11:33–36 (NIV)

There are so many things about God around which we cannot wrap our minds. Aren't you glad? I am so thankful for the things revealed that seem reasonable to me, but I am also comforted that God is high enough above me that I don't understand everything. He is full of mystery and so worthy of praise. Spend some time this morning thinking about the things that you cannot wrap your mind around. Celebrate the greatness of God, who not only has it all figured out but who reigns over all of it!

Invite God to Speak to You Today

"Lord, It's scary to give my life fully to your purposes! As I seek you today, stir my affection for you. Break my heart for the things that break your heart. Give me a hunger to live for you and your purposes. Thank you for moving in mighty ways in my generation. Show me how I can join you in what you are doing today."

Read a Portion of *Spirit Walk*

Read the Interlude, **The Story Line of History**.

Reflect & Respond

1. Can you state in your own words the story line of history?

2. How does the storyline of history help you make sense of what is going on in the world today? In your life?

3. Where does your life fall between being a side character and a protagonist? What would it look life for you to be a protagonist in God's story?

4. In each of our lives there are ways in which we have lived for God's purposes and other ways in which we have lived for our own agendas. Described some ways you have lived for God's purposes.

- Ask the Lord, "Father, how have I lived for your purposes?" Did He bring anything to mind that you had not thought of before?

5. Describe some ways in which you have lived for your own agenda.

- Ask the Lord, "Is there any area of my life where I am currently living for my own agenda instead of your purposes?"

6. What a great day for a prayer of hunger! Re-read the **Prayer of Hunger** in chapter 5. Set aside time to be still before the Lord. Get on your knees or on your face. Cry out to God to awaken your heart to His purposes and His plan for mankind and for you! There is NO GREATER ADVENTURE than walking in relationship with God and being a part of His great story line! After you have spent some time with the Lord, write your own prayer of hunger in the space provided.

DAY 4

Be Still Before the Lord (2 minutes)

Worship the Lord

All this is from God, who through Christ reconciled us to himself and gave us the ministry of reconciliation; that is, in Christ God was reconciling the world to himself, not counting their trespasses against them, and entrusting to us the message of reconciliation. Therefore, we are ambassadors for Christ, God making his appeal through us. We implore you on behalf of Christ, be reconciled to God.
—2 Corinthians 5:18–20

Spend some time thanking the Lord for reconciling you to Himself and for inviting you to be a part of His great plan for mankind. Ask Him to show you how you can partner with Him today!

Invite God to Speak to You Today

"Lord, here I am. I have this one life to live for you, and I don't want to waste it! Empower me today to glorify you, to hunger for you, to surrender to you and to choose you over everything else! You are worthy of my affection and of every day that I live!"

Read a Portion of *Spirit Walk*

Read **The Father's Rescue Van** at the end of Appendix 4.

Reflect & Respond

A lot of times, we don't even know where to start when it comes to partnering with the Father in His mission to rescue the people he loves. Maybe, like so many others, you've gotten sidetracked. You may have gotten distracted fixing up your van. You may have become discouraged because your van isn't as fancy as the other vans out there. Maybe you have been afraid of running out of fuel and being left high and dry. Don't worry! The Lord knows exactly what you need. He will always provide what you need to accomplish HIS mission. Or maybe like so many well-equipped sons, you've been sitting in your perfectly prepared van, but it has been powerless to reach people without the fuel (power) that only your Father can provide. It's been frustrating to see all these cheap vans out there that are more effective at rescuing people than you have been. No matter where you find yourself today, NOW is the time to humbly ask the Father for some fuel and confidently get that van out on the road. God's power always accompanies God's people when they depend on Him to accomplish His purpose! He will not let you down!

1. The Lord has entrusted you with His rescue van. How are you doing stewarding it?

2. What are some ways that you've fixed up your van? Have those investments enabled you to rescue people more effectively or have they actually distracted you from your mission? Or both? Explain.

3. Spend some time asking the Lord for clear direction on how He wants to use YOU in His mission to reconcile all people to Himself. If he brings someone to your mind, ask Him how He wants you to reach out to them. If He puts something on your heart, write it down and make a plan to obey. Share it with a trusted friend who will hold you accountable!

4. The prayer of surrender is the prayer not only to know God's will but to have the courage to do it. I pray that the Lord gives you the courage to pray that prayer whole-heartedly today. Re-read the **Prayer of Surrender** in *Spirit Walk*. Set aside time to wait on the Lord in prayer and write your own prayer of surrender or desperation.

DAY 5

Be Still Before the Lord (2 minutes)

Worship the Lord

The LORD will fulfill his purpose for me; your steadfast love, O LORD, endures forever. Do not forsake the work of your hands. —Psalm 138:8

We have spent a lot of time this week seeking the Lord and meditating on His purposes. Today, worship the Lord that He is faithful to love you and has never given up on His purposes in your life!

Invite God to Speak to You Today

"Lord, here I am again. I have this one life to live for you, and I don't want to waste it! Empower me today to glorify you, to hunger for you, to surrender to you and to choose you over everything else! You are worthy of my affection and of every day that I live!"

Bible Study

Select a Scripture from this week's reading to study, and write the full verse(s) below.

1. Turn to the verse in your Bible and read it in the context of the full chapter. Does reading it in context, or in another translation, add to your understanding of this passage? If so, how?

2. Look up any key words that may help you gain a deeper understanding of the passage.

3. Ask the Lord, "What do you specifically want to speak to me through this passage today?"

4. Does this passage challenge any assumptions you have about "Living according to the Holy Spirit?"

5. What truth does this Scripture reveal about God, and how can it move you to worship Him today?

6. What does this Scripture reveal about you and/or humanity in general?

7. Ask the Lord, "Would you show me if there is any wrong belief or sin in my heart that has kept me from living in conformity with this Scripture?"

8. What practical steps of obedience will you take today in response to this passage?

9. Who will you tell something you learned from this passage?

10. Write a prayer in your journal thanking God for what He is teaching you and asking Him for the courage to surrender to Him completely.

Session 5 | THE DEEP WORK

DAY 1

Be Still Before the Lord (2 minutes)

Remember the purpose of this time is to fix our eyes and affection on God alone. By this time, I pray that being still before the Lord is becoming a more natural part of your day. Make it your goal to quiet yourself in the Lord's presence several times today. Consider setting an alarm on your phone to remind you or making it a part of your daily routine. Pause for a couple of minutes each day before you walk into the house after work or each time you drive up to your favorite store. It could be your routine to turn your attention to the Lord for a few minutes every time you are stopped at a red light or before you turn on your computer for the day.

Worship the Lord

> *Oh sing to the Lord a new song;*
> *sing to the Lord, all the earth!*
> *Sing to the Lord, bless his name;*
> *tell of his salvation from day to day.*
> *Declare his glory among the nations,*
> *his marvelous works among all the peoples!*
> —Psalm 96:1–3

The Lord is God over all peoples and all nations. He is doing miraculous things in our day all over the globe. Take some time to read Psalm 96 aloud. Say among the nations, "The Lord Reigns!"

Invite God to Speak to You Today

"Father, I draw near to you today. Draw near to me as I wait on You!"

Read a Portion of *Spirit Walk*

Read Chapter 6, S.W.A.P.—Wait on God in Prayer through The Sweet Honeymoon.

Reflect & Respond

1. Are you the kind of person to whom God would entrust the power of His Spirit? God's entrusting His Spirit is not based on the height of your spiritual attainment but rather on the posture of your heart. What needs to change within you to refine that posture?

2. How does viewing a longer getaway with God as a honeymoon help you in thinking about how to meet with Him?

3. Have you ever gotten away with the Lord for an extended amount of time? If so, what was fruit of that time in your relationship with the Lord—in your life or ministry?

DAY 2

Be Still Before the Lord (2 minutes)

Worship the Lord

I love the LORD, for he heard my voice; he heard my cry for mercy. Because he turned his ear to me, I will call on him as long as I live. —Psalm 116:1–2 (NIV)

Today spend some time expressing gratitude to the Lord that He hears you when you cry out to Him, and that He is moved by your prayers. How incredible that the almighty, eternal God would set His attention and affection on the likes of us! Recall past times when God has heard your cry and responded to your need. Write down a few examples that come to mind. Worship the Lord for His goodness to you.

Invite God to Speak to You Today

"Father, I draw near to you today. Draw near to me as I wait on You!"

Read a Portion of *Spirit Walk*

Read Chapter 6, **Frequent Forays—Staying Filled** through the end of the chapter.

Reflect & Respond

1. How does viewing daily quiet times as a date with God help you in thinking about how to meet with Him?

2. George Mueller said that the goal of his quiet time was to get his soul happy in the Lord. Is this the way you have approached time with God in the past? How would your daily time with God change if this were your goal?

3. Now that you have scheduled your SWAPmeet, how do you envision it unfolding? Will you do it by yourself or with friends?

4. If with a group, discuss with your group when and where your daily quiet time will unfold. How can you set up to designate it as a date with God? If alone, how can you build a schedule and hold yourself accountable?

DAY 3

Daily SWAPmeet

Turn to Appendix 1 in *Spirit Walk (Special Edition)*. Read the section entitled **Daily SWAP**.

Our purpose this week is to develop the habit of waiting on God in prayer, and to cultivate our relationship with Him through spending unhurried time seeking His face. Use the outline below, from *Spirit Walk* to work through your Daily SWAPmeet with the Lord.

Invite God to Speak to You Today.

Read through a Psalm.
Remember, you are not merely reading a dead book. You are reading the living word of God with the Holy Spirit as your guide. Like a child who reads a book with their parent, pause when you don't understand something and ask the Lord what it means. Interrupt the reading to tell Him when something grabs your attention and let Him interrupt your progress to share His thoughts with you. The Word of God is ALIVE because the Spirit of God LIVES to reveal truth to you through it!

Read a passage from the New Testament.
Take time to be still before the Lord and ask Him to convict you, to encourage you and to reveal Himself to you through His word.

Read through a Proverb in the same way. (Optional)

Journal.
As you work through Scriptures, spend unhurried time in prayer, reflecting on what you have read and writing down your thoughts and prayers.

Pray through the S.W.A.P. acronym.
Surrender control to the Lord. **Wait** on Him. **Avoid** sin. Confess anything He brings to mind and immediately repent. **Pursue** the promptings of the Spirit, immediately obeying anything the Lord prompts you to do while you are spending time with Him.

Pray through your normal prayer list.
If you have never written a list of things to pray for regularly, do so now. Ask the Lord to guide you in this process. You may start the process by praying:

- "Father, what do you want me to ask you for?"

- "Who do you want me to pray for on a regular basis?"

- "How do you want me to pray for my spouse?"

- "How do you want me to pray for my parents or children?"

- "Lord, give me a heart for my coworkers, neighbors, church and nation? How do you want me to pray for these on a regular basis?"

- "Is there a missionary, ministry or people-group that You specifically want me to pray for on a regular basis?"

Humbly and confidently bring these requests before your loving Father. He is so generous, and He loves you!

Rise in faith that He is filling you and continue to turn your attention to Him throughout the day.

DAY 4

Daily SWAPmeet

How would you feel if you were on a date with someone you love, and they were hurrying through the motions so they could get on with their day? Imagine them reading through a list of questions for you, but never pausing to let you answer. Now imagine that you handed them a heartfelt letter. They read it quickly, then folded it up and put it away, but didn't say anything in response. Instead they wrapped up your time together by giving you a list of To Do's. To their credit, they followed it up with a, "Please, and I love you." Would you feel honored? No! You would likely be offended or grieved. Hasn't the Lord been so gracious with us! Let's not treat the Holy Spirit that way today! Instead, slow down. Give Him your full attention. Relax with the Lord. Enjoy His presence. Savor His word. Discover something new about Him. Let your affection for Him be stirred.

Today, work through the SWAPmeet again, using the outline below as your guide, but feel free to let the Holy Spirit guide your time with Him in any way He desires.

Read through a Psalm.

Read a passage from the New Testament.

Read through a Proverb in the same way. (Optional)

Journal.

Pray through the S.W.A.P. acronym.

Pray through your normal prayer list.

Rise in faith.

DAY 5

Be Still Before the Lord (2 minutes)

Worship the Lord

And without faith it is impossible to please him, for whoever would draw near to God must believe that he exists and that he rewards those who seek him.

—Hebrews 11:6

What a privilege to draw near to God—the almighty, eternal, uncreated ruler of all things. We draw near with the help of the Holy Spirit because of Christ's sacrifice that covered our unworthiness. And what an encouragement to know that when we draw near in faith, God does not hide himself from us! Instead, He is pleased and rewards us. Let that word encourage your heart today as you seek the Lord in His word. Spend some time worshipping through prayer and expressing your gratitude to God for rewarding you when you have sought Him in the past. Thank Him, by faith, that He will reveal Himself to you afresh today!

Invite God to Speak to You Today

"Father, I draw near to you today. Draw near to me as I seek you in your word."

Bible Study

Select a Scripture from this week's reading to study, and write the full verse(s) below.

1. Turn to the verse in your Bible and read it in the context of the full chapter. Does reading it in context, or in another translation, add to your understanding of this passage? If so, how?

2. Look up any key words that may help you gain a deeper understanding of the passage.

3. Ask the Lord, "What do you specifically want to speak to me through this passage today?"

4. Does this passage challenge any assumptions you have about "Living according to the Holy Spirit?"

5. What truth does this Scripture reveal about God, and how can it move you to worship Him today?

6. What does this Scripture reveal about you and/or humanity in general?

7. Ask the Lord, "Would you show me if there is any wrong belief or sin in my heart that has kept me from living in conformity with this Scripture?"

8. What practical steps of obedience will you take today in response to this passage?

9. Who will you tell something you learned from this passage?

10. Write a prayer in your journal thanking God for what He is teaching you and asking Him for the courage to surrender to Him completely.

Session 5 NOTES **The Deep Work**

AVOIDING SIN AND LETTING GOD ROOT OUT ALL UNRIGHTEOUSNESS

DAY 1

Be Still Before the Lord (2 minutes)

Worship the Lord

> *And I will betroth you to me forever. I will betroth you to me in righteousness and in justice, in steadfast love and in mercy. I will betroth you to me in faithfulness. And you shall know the LORD.*
> —Hosea 2:19–20

Turn to Hosea 2 in your Bible and read the whole chapter. Take some time to praise the Lord for the ways He has been patient with you and pursued your heart when you were forgetful and unfaithful.

Think about what it is like to adore a small child or first love. You look at them and let them captivate your full attention. You are fully present in the moment to enjoy their personality and beauty. ADORE the Lord like that today! Let yourself be fully present with Him and captivated by the beauty and goodness of our God.

Invite God to Speak to You Today

"Father, I don't want to grieve your Spirit. It breaks my heart to know that I have grieved you. Shine your light in every single room in my heart as I meet with you today. Expose every area of darkness and root it out of my life completely."

Read a Portion of *Spirit Walk*

Read Chapter 7, **S.W.A.P.—Avoid Sin and Let God Root Out All Unrighteousness** through **Vessels of Use For God.**

Reflect & Respond

1. Read Ephesians 4:30 in *Spirit Walk*. Chances are you can easily recall a time when you experienced grief. Maybe the grief came from the loss of a treasured relationship or a loved one or as the result of a bad decision, life change, or just a chemical imbalance. Whatever it was, describe a specific time when you were deeply grieved.

   • How does it make you feel to know you have grieved the Holy Spirit of God?

2. Re-read **2 Timothy 2:20–22** in *Spirit Walk*. According to this passage, why is it important to clean sin out of our lives?

3. Can you think of any ways in which you have gradually been desensitized to sin? Are there things you once felt were sinful, but you've gradually accepted them. Or maybe there are question-able things you do that you would not allow your children to do. According to God's Word, is it still sinful?

4. Read through the list of eleven sins Paul highlights in Ephesians 4:17–5:21. Has one of these struck a nerve with you? If not, consider another specific sin struggle in your life.

   • What needs to be put off? How do you plan to put it off?

   • What needs to change in your thinking?

   • What is the "holy opposite" you need to put on?

5. Has God taken you through these steps in overcoming past struggles with sin? How can your past experience encourage you in choosing to walk this path with the Lord today?

DAY 2

Be Still Before the Lord (2 minutes)

Worship the Lord

"And I will give you a new heart, and a new spirit I will put within you. And I will remove the heart of stone from your flesh and give you a heart of flesh. And I will put my Spirit within you, and cause you to walk in my statutes and be careful to obey my rules." —Ezekiel 36:26–27

Make a list of some ways that the Holy Spirit has moved you to follow after God. Include specific sins that the Lord has given you victory over. Thank the Lord for convicting you of sin and for empowering you to walk in victory instead of allowing your sin to utterly destroy you like you deserve.

Invite God to Speak to You Today

"Father, I don't want to grieve your Spirit. It breaks my heart to know that I have grieved you. Shine your light in every single room in my heart as I meet with you today. Expose every area of darkness and root it out of my life completely."

Read a Portion of *Spirit Walk*

Chapter 7, **Every Revival Is a Refining Moment** through **Pure, Undivided Devotion**.

Let's deal honestly with ourselves and with the Lord, today. Remember, He is patient with us. His CONVICTION is the kindness of God to expose the things that are threatening to destroy us and to draw us back to Himself so He can empower us to walk in victory.

"If say, 'Surely the darkness will hide me and day become night around me,' even the darkness will not be dark to you. The night will shine like the day, for darkness is as light to you." —Psalm 139:11–12

Reflect & Respond

1. Ask yourself, "At this point in my life, do I prefer the passing delights of sin more than the enduring delight of holiness?" What is your honest answer?

   • In what ways have you chosen the comfortable shadows of darkness as opposed to the discomforting exposure of the light in the past?

   • In what ways are you currently choosing comfortable darkness over walking in the light?

2. If your spouse were faithful to you 364 days a year or 23 hours every day, how would that make you feel? How does this impact the way you think about grieving the Holy Spirit?

3. "The proper emphasis of a holy lifestyle is not to see how close to the line between temptation and sin you can get, but how far from that line you can remain." Is there an area in your life in which you have tried to walk close to "the line?" What are some changes you can make to instead flee from temptation?

4. Paul gives instructions that those chosen as leaders in the church must be "above reproach" (1 Timothy 3:2), that is, not only avoid sinning, but also avoid things that might simply appear to be wrong. This is a requirement for leaders, but it is something to which each of us should aspire. What are some steps you can take to avoid even the perception of sinning?

5. Are there some sins you are "dabbling" in? Write them down on a sheet of paper and lay the paper out as a sacrifice to the Lord. Ask your loving heavenly Father to help you enjoy and desire intimacy with Him more than the fleeting pleasure these things. Then burn the paper like a burnt offering. Go and sin no more.

DAY 3

Be Still Before the Lord (2 minutes)

Worship the Lord

Keep your life free from love of money, and be content with what you have, for he has said, "I will never leave you nor forsake you." So we can confidently say, "The Lord is my helper; I will not fear; what can man do to me?" —Hebrews 13:5–6

Rich or poor, all of us are tempted to love comfort, security and indulgence and to put our hope in these things. But unlike the world, our joy isn't contingent upon our circumstances or our bank account. Our hope is in God's presence with us, and His Spirit in us guarantees an eternal inheritance, the value of which we cannot begin to fathom (Ephesians 1:14). Spend some time today worshipping the Lord by thanking Him for all the ways He provides for you. Ask Him, "Father, have I grieved you by loving money?" Confess any discontentment, love of money or fear of man that the Holy Spirit reveals. Then ask Him, "Lord, how are you providing for me today?" Make a list of the things that come to mind and pause to thank Him for each one. God is so generous with us!

Invite God to Speak to You Today

"Father, I don't want to grieve your Spirit. It breaks my heart to know that I have grieved you. Shine your light in every single room in my heart as I meet with you today. Expose every area of darkness and root it out of my life completely."

Read a Portion of *Spirit Walk*

Read Chapter 7, **Expose Sin and Receive Forgiveness** through **Sweet Restoration**.

Reflect & Respond

1. Re-read **John 3:19–21** in chapter 7. As the Lord convicts you of certain sins, write them down (in code or shorthand, if you would like) and confess them to your loving and compassionate heavenly Father. Confession is simply agreeing with God about your sin.

If we confess our sins, He is faithful and just to forgive us our sins and to cleanse us from all unrighteousness. —1 John 1:9

2. Select one item from your "sin list" that the Father is speaking to you most strongly to change. (Or perhaps it is something you even resisted writing down.) What is the "holy opposite" of that? How can you begin to "put off" the sin and "put on" the "holy opposite?"

3. Write down a scripture to memorize to help you "renew your mind" so that it is easier to "put off" the sin and "put on" the "holy opposite."

4. Are there stumbling blocks you need to remove to help you avoid that sin and walk in holiness? If so, list those and consider how you will remove them.

DAY 4

Be Still Before the Lord (2 minutes)

Worship the Lord

All Scripture is God-breathed and is useful for teaching, rebuking, correcting and training in righteousness, so that the servant of God may be thoroughly equipped for every good work. —2 Timothy 3:16–17 (NIV)

There is no one holy like the LORD;
there is no one besides you;
there is no Rock like our God

—1 Samuel 2:2 (NIV)

Think of specific examples when the Lord has spoken to you through His word. Worship God for giving us the Bible and making it alive to us by His Spirit! How incredible that a 2000-year-old book written by forty authors on three continents over a 1500-year-period still speaks so powerfully and relevantly to our lives today! How great is our God! Who is like Him?

Invite God to Speak to You Today

"Father, thank you for the work you have already been doing in my heart this week. Continue to expose any area of darkness in my heart that needs to be rooted out. Teach me how to walk in your victory over sin and unrighteousness."

Read a Portion of *Spirit Walk*

Read Chapter 7, **The Life-Giving Power of Confession** through the end of the chapter.

Reflect & Respond

1. Is there something you need to confess to a trusted group of same-sex disciples so that you can be free from it? What is it?

- Make a plan to obey the conviction of the Holy Spirit from number 1, right now. Write down the names of people whom you can trust to journey with you in overcoming this sin. Contact them to get together before moving on to the next question.

2. Is there something you need to confess to someone you have offended or been offended by to forgive and be forgiven in order to avoid a root of bitterness?

   • Make a plan to obey immediately. Consider how wide the confession should be (generally, as wide as the offense) and talk to your group leader or another trusted leader if you need help discerning how to move forward in confessing to others. Remember, the goal is not just to get it off your chest. Your confession which makes you feel better may create great trauma for someone else who does not even currently know you sinned against them. Confess carefully and with good counsel.

3. Describe each of these three ways that sin is confronted in our lives. What is the source of each of these? Give an example of each from your own life.

   • Conviction—

   • Commendation (rationalization)—

   • Condemnation—

4. Read back through the **Weslayan prayers** in chapter 7, allowing the Holy Spirit to speak to you as you do. Do any of these questions particularly pierce your heart or make you uncomfortable? Why do you think they impact you in this way?

5. Jesus said:

   "For if you forgive others their trespasses, your heavenly Father will also forgive you, but if you do not forgive others their trespasses, neither will your Father forgive your trespasses." —Matthew 6:14–15

   Is there someone you need to forgive?

DAY 5

Be Still Before the Lord (2 minutes)

Worship the Lord

Therefore, my beloved, as you have always obeyed, so now, not only as in my presence but much more in my absence, work out your own salvation with fear and trembling, for it is God who works in you, both to will and to work for his good pleasure. —Philippians 2:12–13

Worship the Lord today for how He works in you to transform you by His power and goodness! Praise the Lord that you don't have to work out your salvation in your own strength, but freely receive from the Holy Spirit as you live in relationship with Him!

Invite God to Speak to You Today

"God, I love you, and I want to love you even more! Forgive me for living in my own strength and for going my own way. Work in my heart to root out everything that does not please you and fill me afresh with your Spirit as I seek your face today!"

Bible Study

Select a Scripture from this week's reading to study, and write the full verse(s) below.

1. Turn to the verse in your Bible and read it in the context of the full chapter. Does reading it in context, or in another translation, add to your understanding of this passage? If so, how?

2. Look up any key words that may help you gain a deeper understanding of the passage.

3. Ask the Lord, "What do you specifically want to speak to me through this passage today?"

4. Does this passage challenge any assumptions you have about "Living according to the Holy Spirit?"

5. What truth does this Scripture reveal about God, and how can it move you to worship Him today?

6. What does this Scripture reveal about you and/or humanity in general?

7. Ask the Lord, "Would you show me if there is any wrong belief or sin in my heart that has kept me from living in conformity with this Scripture?"

8. What practical steps of obedience will you take today in response to this passage?

9. Who will you tell something you learned from this passage?

10. Write a prayer in your journal thanking God for what He is teaching you and asking Him for the courage to surrender to Him completely.

Avoiding Sin and Letting God Root Out All Unrighteousness

PURSUING THE PROMPTINGS OF THE HOLY SPIRIT

DAY 1

Be Still Before the Lord (2 minutes)

Worship the Lord

There are no words to adequately describe the glory of our God. Angels encircle the throne constantly declaring His praises. Take some time to read the following Scriptures and meditate on His greatness today!

> In the year that King Uzziah died I saw the Lord sitting upon a throne, high and lifted up; and the train[a] of his robe filled the temple. Above him stood the seraphim. Each had six wings: with two he covered his face, and with two he covered his feet, and with two he flew. 3 And one called to another and said:
>
> > "Holy, holy, holy is the Lord of hosts;
> > the whole earth is full of his glory!"
>
> And the foundations of the thresholds shook at the voice of him who called, and the house was filled with smoke.
>
> —Isaiah 6:1–4

> Then I looked, and I heard around the throne and the living creatures and the elders the voice of many angels, numbering myriads of myriads and thousands of thousands, saying with a loud voice,
>
> > "Worthy is the Lamb who was slain,
> > to receive power and wealth and wisdom and might
> > and honor and glory and blessing!"
>
> And I heard every creature in heaven and on earth and under the earth and in the sea, and all that is in them, saying,
>
> > "To him who sits on the throne and to the Lamb
> > be blessing and honor and glory and might forever and ever!"
>
> —Revelation 5:11–13

Above the vault over their heads was what looked like a throne of lapis lazuli, and high above on the throne was a figure like that of a man. I saw that from what appeared to be his waist up he looked like glowing metal, as if full of fire, and that from there down he looked like fire; and brilliant light surrounded him. Like the appearance of a rainbow in the clouds on a rainy day, so was the radiance around him.

This was the appearance of the likeness of the glory of the LORD. When I saw it, I fell facedown, and I heard the voice of one speaking.　　　—Ezekiel 1:26–28

Invite God to Speak to You Today

"Lord Jesus! More than anything else I want to be filled with your Spirit to accomplish YOUR purposes. Help me to walk in the good works you have already prepared for me. Help me let your light shine and not hide it under a bushel. I want YOU to be in complete control. I want to live for YOUR purposes, not my own. Fill me completely, I pray, and I will follow where YOU lead!"

Read a Portion of *Spirit Walk*

Read Chapter 8, **S.W.A.P.—Pursue the Promptings of the Spirit** through **Rely on the Power and Guidance of the Spirit Each Moment.**

Reflect & Respond

1. **If you are aware that the Holy Spirit is completely filling you right now**, take as much time and space as needed to journal all that you are thinking, feeling, and experiencing. How does this impact your desire to give him free access in the future? **(If you are not aware of His filling, go on to question 2.)**

2. **If you are NOT aware that the Holy Spirit is completely filling you right now, don't panic.** Take time to examine these things:

   - Are you completely surrendered to all you know of God's will and Word?

   - Have you invited Him to root out sin in your life and waited patiently for Him to do all that is needed in this area?

   - Where necessary, have you confessed your sins to others and made restitution as needed? Are you actively avoiding sin, having removed frequent stumbling blocks and enlisting others to hold you accountable as necessary?

   - Are you filling your mind with God's Word?

If the answer to any of the above is "no," I plead with you not to resist the Holy Spirit but to come to him humbly and to surrender in every way. Pray this way, "Lord, I am completely Yours. Have Your way in me. I want all of You and I give You all of me."

If the answer to all of the above is "yes," still don't panic. We know according to Luke 11:13 that the Father is eager to give the Holy Spirit to those who ask Him. Simply step out in faith that God has answered your request (assuming you asked him per **The Spirit Ask** in chapter 8) and do the next thing you know He wants you to do, being sensitive to any ways that He may prompt you to minister to others around you.

DAY 2

Be Still Before the Lord (2 minutes)

Worship the Lord

"And I tell you, ask, and it will be given to you; seek, and you will find; knock, and it will be opened to you. For everyone who asks receives, and the one who seeks finds, and to the one who knocks it will be opened. What father among you, if his son asks for a fish, will instead of a fish give him a serpent; or if he asks for an egg, will give him a scorpion? If you then, who are evil, know how to give good gifts to your children, how much more will the heavenly Father give the Holy Spirit to those who ask him!" —Luke 11:9–13

On the last day of the feast, the great day, Jesus stood up and cried out, "If anyone thirsts, let him come to me and drink. Whoever believes in me, as the Scripture has said, 'Out of his heart will flow rivers of living water.'" Now this he said about the Spirit, whom those who believed in him were to receive, for as yet the Spirit had not been given, because Jesus was not yet glorified.

—John 7:37–39

Isn't it good to know that the Father is not holding out on you? Walk through the steps of the S.W.A.P. process in prayer. Ask the Spirit of God to fill you afresh today. Receive Him by faith and worship God with thanksgiving, knowing that the Father delights to answer your prayer!

Invite God to Speak to You Today

"Lord Jesus! More than anything else I want to be filled with your Spirit to accomplish YOUR purposes. Help me to walk in the good works you have already prepared for me. Help me let your light shine and not hide it under a bushel. I want YOU to be in complete control. I want to live for YOUR purposes, not my own. Fill me completely, I pray, and I will follow where YOU lead!"

Read a Portion of *Spirit Walk*

Read Chapter 8, **When He Fills You, He Speaks to You** through **Promptings for Your Good As Well.**

Reflect & Respond

1. Why is it important to know and to abide in God's Word and to have His word abiding in us in order to recognize the Holy Spirit's promptings?

2. List any fears or hesitations you have as you consider following the promptings of the Holy Spirit. Make a note also of any scriptures that come to mind that relate to these fears.

3. Look back over your list. Pray and ask our loving Father to help you trust and submit to Him in these areas.

4. Consider Psalm 16:4 and Psalm 16:11. Have you bartered for anything other than the God of the Bible? If so, what do you need to do to reverse that barter, to trade what is life-stealing for what is life-giving?

5. How have you been surprised by joy in saying "yes" to a prompting to which you wanted to say "no?" Share your experience with others to encourage them.

DAY 3

Be Still Before the Lord (2 minutes)

Worship the Lord

There are different kinds of gifts, but the same Spirit distributes them. There are different kinds of service, but the same Lord. There are different kinds of working, but in all of them and in everyone it is the same God at work.

—1 Corinthians 12:4–7 (NIV)

Express gratitude to the Lord today that He gives spiritual gifts to His children. Specifically thank Him for a spiritual gift you have received. Worship Him for the ways He has used you to edify the body of Christ and the ways He will use you in the future! Spend some time thanking God for the spiritual gifts He has given to others in the body of Christ. Write down a few specific ways the Lord has strengthened or blessed you through someone else's spiritual gifting.

Invite God to Speak to You Today

"Lord Jesus! More than anything else I want to be filled with your Spirit to accomplish YOUR purposes. Help me to walk in the good works you have already prepared for me. Help me let your light shine and not hide it under a bushel. I want YOU to be in complete control. I want to live for YOUR purposes, not my own. Fill me completely, I pray, and I will follow where YOU lead!"

Read a Portion of *Spirit Walk*

Read Chapter 8, **To Stay Full of the Spirit, Keep Saying Yes** through the end of the Chapter.

Reflect & Respond

1. Have you been surprised by the answer to the greatest sign of the Spirit-led life—being prompted to speak the Word of God boldly and with love?

   • Examine your life. How have you experienced boldness in telling others about Jesus?

- Does worship regularly flow from your heart?

- Do you relate to others in a loving way?

2. What other promptings of the Spirit described in this chapter were a surprise to you? What felt refreshing when you read it?

3. According to Galatians 5:22–24, how the Spirit Walk lead to a transformed character and life?

DAY 4

Be Still Before the Lord (2 minutes)

Worship the Lord

"My sheep listen to my voice; I know them, and they follow me. I give them eternal life, and they shall never perish; no one will snatch them out of my hand. My Father, who has given them to me, is greater than all; no one can snatch them out of my Father's hand. I and the Father are one." —John 10:27–30

Take a moment and turn to John chapter 10 in your Bible. Read through the chapter and worship the Lord in an unhurried way. Meditate on the faithfulness of God to pursue you, to redeem you, to give you eternal, abundant life and to enable you to follow Him and to hear His voice. Who is like our God? There is none mighty like God! No one can fathom the depths of His great love, and He has set His love upon YOU!

Invite God to Speak to You Today

"Father, I want to know You better and to love You more. Please reveal Yourself to me. Show me Your glory as I seek You today!"

Read a Portion of *Spirit Walk*

Read the **Conclusion**.

Reflect & Respond

1. Consider how your understanding of the Holy Spirit and His role in the Christian life has changed over the past several weeks or months.

2. How have you been challenged to surrender to the Holy Spirit in new ways?

3. How have you seen the fruit of the Spirit grow in your life over the course of this study?

4. Have you taken new steps of obedience to partner with God in His mission as you've grown in your walk with the Holy Spirit?

> **This is the conclusion of today's study, but the BEGINNING of living:**
> **for God's purposes**
> **by His power,**
> **responding to His promptings**
> **to partner with Him in what He is already doing.**

Who can you partner with for mutual encouragement and accountability in this journey? Jot down 8–10 names of people who might be interested and make a plan to talk to each person this week, if you have not already. After forming your "intrepid band," together make a plan for how you will encourage one another and hold one another accountable. Consider using Wesley's accountability questions.

DAY 5

Be Still Before the Lord (2 minutes)

Worship the Lord

When the Spirit of truth comes, he will guide you into all the truth, for he will not speak on his own authority, but whatever he hears he will speak, and he will declare to you the things that are to come. He will glorify me, for he will take what is mine and declare it to you.
—John 16:13–14

Make a list of some things the Lord has taught you over the course of this study and worship the Lord for sending His Holy Spirit to teach us, to council us, to reveal the Father and Son to us and to lead us into all truth.

Invite God to Speak to You Today

"Father, I want to know what You are doing in my generation, and I want to bring great glory to You with my life. Show me Your will and how I can serve that. Make yourself famous through me. Father, speak to me through your word today as I seek your face!"

Bible Study

Select a Scripture from this week's reading to study, and write the full verse(s) below.

1. Turn to the verse in your Bible and read it in the context of the full chapter. Does reading it in context, or in another translation, add to your understanding of this passage? If so, how?

2. Look up any key words that may help you gain a deeper understanding of the passage.

3. Ask the Lord, "What do you specifically want to speak to me through this passage today?"

4. Does this passage challenge any assumptions you have about "Living according to the Holy Spirit?"

5. What truth does this Scripture reveal about God, and how can it move you to worship Him today?

6. What does this Scripture reveal about you and/or humanity in general?

7. Ask the Lord, "Would you show me if there is any wrong belief or sin in my heart that has kept me from living in conformity with this Scripture?"

8. What practical steps of obedience will you take today in response to this passage?

9. Who will you tell something you learned from this passage?

10. Write a prayer in your journal thanking God for what He is teaching you and asking Him for the courage to surrender to Him completely.

Session **8**

STAYING THE COURSE— KEEPING STEP WITH THE HOLY TRAILBLAZER

DAY 1

Over the next week, we will take time each day to meet with the Lord and walk through a daily SWAPmeet of our own.

Remember, daily time with the Lord is NOT a formula. It's not a burdensome obligation. The God of heaven does not need you to do a rain dance to get His attention, and you could not impress Him with YOUR righteous acts no matter how hard you tried.

The Father has clothed you in the righteousness of Christ Jesus and adopted you as His beloved child. He longs to reveal Himself to you and to meet you intimately each day. The reason we seek the Lord daily is to invest in our relationship with Him.

Developing the spiritual discipline of meeting with the Lord daily is an act of LOVE. Just like maintaining a healthy marriage requires setting aside time to connect intentionally with your spouse, maintaining a healthy spiritual walk requires that we intentionally create space in our lives for prioritizing our relationship with the Holy Spirit.

In the same way that few of us successfully implement healthy workout habits or diets without first making a plan for how we will succeed, few people really invest in their relationship with the Lord without having a plan in place. Have you ever decided you wanted to lose weight or to get into better shape without having a firm plan for how you will proceed? I have. Do you know what changed about my daily habits? Basically nothing! I made a handful of healthy decisions, but made no real progress toward life transformation. I had a desire to lose weight or eat healthier foods, but without a firm plan, I just defaulted into the same old unhealthy patterns. Having a plan helps us stay the course when we get distracted or feel disinterested. So let's make a plan.

Develop Your Own Pattern for a Daily SWAPmeet

Your relationship with the Lord is unique. It has its own fingerprint and its own DNA, so set aside some time today to develop a structure that empowers you to consistently spend time with the Lord. Feel free to turn to **Appendix 1**, and use the Daily SWAP as a guide. As you read the outline, underline each activity that you envision including in your own routine of meeting with the Lord. Then, using the space provided, or in your personal journal, write a plan for how you will structure your daily SWAPmeets.

Example—

- Activity 1: Read a Psalm
- Purpose for this activity—Stir my heart to love the Lord. Center my thoughts
- on God and worship Him.
- How often do you want to do this? (daily? weekly?) 4 times a week
- How much time do you plan on devoting to this section each day?
- 3–10 minutes
- How can you keep this activity from becoming monotonous? *Switch up what I'm reading. Read aloud or sing. Remember that I'm reading it with the Holy Spirit, like a child reading with their Father. Invite Him to join me in reading it each day and pause to ask Him what He thinks and to worship.*

My Daily S.W.A.P. plan

Activity 1:

- Purpose for this activity—

- How often do you want to do this?

- How much time do you plan on devoting to this section each day?

- How can you keep this activity from becoming monotonous?

Activity 2:

- Purpose for this activity—

- How often do you want to do this?

- How much time do you plan on devoting to this section each day?

- How can you keep this activity from becoming monotonous?

Activity 3:

- Purpose for this activity—

- How often do you want to do this?

- How much time do you plan on devoting to this section each day?

- How can you keep this activity from becoming monotonous?

Activity 4:

- Purpose for this activity—

- How often do you want to do this?

- How much time do you plan on devoting to this section each day?

- How can you keep this activity from becoming monotonous?

Activity 5:

- Purpose for this activity—

- How often do you want to do this?

- How much time do you plan on devoting to this section each day?

- How can you keep this activity from becoming monotonous?

Activity 6:

- Purpose for this activity—

- How often do you want to do this?

- How much time do you plan on devoting to this section each day?

- How can you keep this activity from becoming monotonous?

How do you plan to wrap up your time with the Lord each day?

What practical steps can you take to turn your attention back to the Lord and check in with Him throughout your day?

DAYS 2–5

Now that you've developed a plan for meeting with the Lord daily, put it into practice. Use your new Daily SWAPmeet plan as a guide for your "quiet time" each day.

Remember, spiritual disciplines and processes are useful tools, but they remain powerless and often burdensome apart from the Holy Spirit breathing life into them. Take time before you proceed to ask the Lord to breathe life into this process for you. Ask Him to meet with you, to lead you into truth, to convict you of sin, to encourage you and to empower you as you seek Him each day!

Before you are done each day, make a plan for when you will get alone with the Lord the following day.

Staying the Course—Keeping Step with the Holy Trailblazer

STICK WITH IT!

You've done some of the hard work in this study by taking your first steps on your Spirit Walk, but now is the time to learn the discipline of long obedience from life-long pursuit and to reap the rewards of the joy that comes from that kind of regular intimacy with the Lord.

Set apart time each day to express your love for the Lord by prioritizing time with Him. Use your Daily SWAPmeet plan to keep you on track. Surrender afresh to Him each day and ask Him to fill you afresh so you can live for His purposes with His power. Start today by meditating on John 14:15–21.

> *"If you love me, you will keep my commandments. And I will ask the Father, and he will give you another Helper, to be with you forever, even the Spirit of truth, whom the world cannot receive, because it neither sees him nor knows him. You know him, for he dwells with you and will be in you.*
>
> *"I will not leave you as orphans; I will come to you. Yet a little while and the world will see me no more, but you will see me. Because I live, you also will live. In that day you will know that I am in my Father, and you in me, and I in you. Whoever has my commandments and keeps them, he it is who loves me. And he who loves me will be loved by my Father, and I will love him and manifest myself to him."*
>
> —John 14:15–21

As fellow travelers on this path, we (the authors) leave you with this benediction and encourage you to pray this for yourself:

Father, thank you for sending your Son to pay my debt, to bridge the impossible gulf between us. Thank you for loving me and adopting me as your own. Lord Jesus, thank you for sending your Holy Spirit to me. Thank you that you did not leave me as an orphan, but you came to me by your Spirit and make yourself known to me day by day. Thank you that He makes the Word of God alive to me. Thank you that He convicts me of sin and empowers me to walk in victory over the schemes of the evil one. Thank you for enabling me to recognize His promptings. And thank you for clothing me with power from on high and appointing me as a minister of reconciliation while I live here on earth.

I do not want to squander this privilege, Lord. I want to walk with the Holy Spirit so that I may know you. I do not want to waste my life. I want to live for your purposes. I don't want to toil in vain to do your will. I want to be filled with your power! I want to S.W.A.P. my control for yours. Lord, would you empower me daily to take up my cross, to crucify my flesh, and to surrender unconditionally to your Holy Spirit as my guide? Would you stir my heart with a passion for your purposes in the earth and strengthen my resolve, so that I do not harden my heart, and grieve your Holy Spirit. And Father, would you fill me completely with your Holy Spirit today, and give me a steadfast heart, I pray, so that I might persevere on this journey with You.

In the mighty and powerful name of Jesus Christ, Amen.

CPSIA information can be obtained
at www.ICGtesting.com
Printed in the USA
BVHW050237231220
595987BV00004B/25

9 781645 083351